GEO

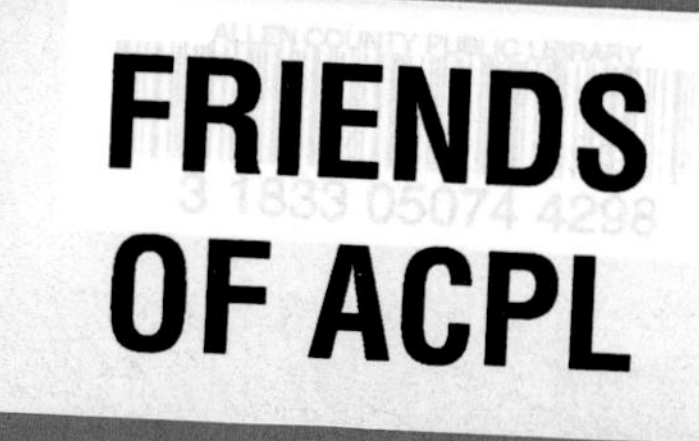
FRIENDS
OF ACPL

P9-DZA-299

Step-by-Step CRAFTS for FALL

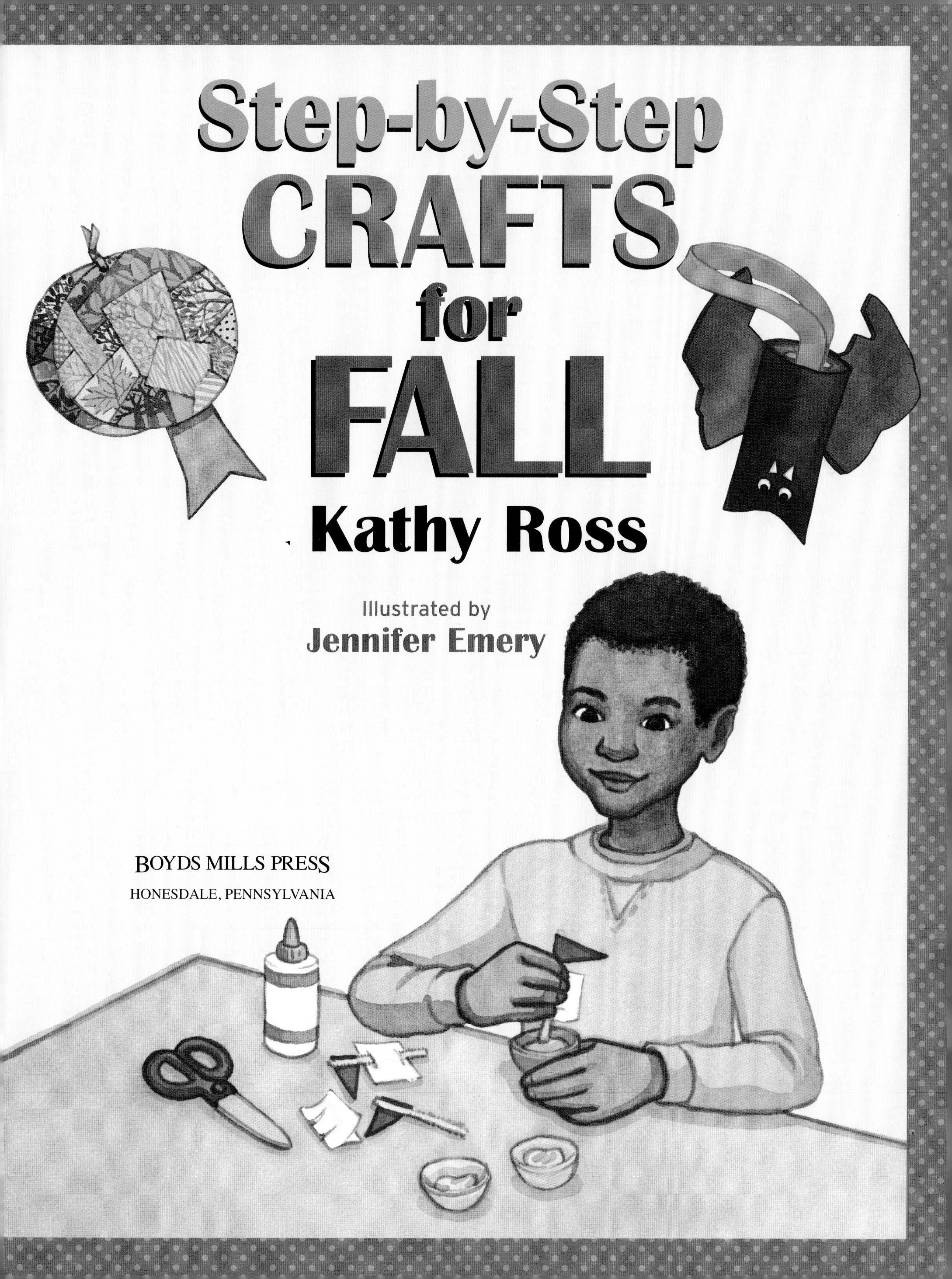

Step-by-Step CRAFTS for FALL

Kathy Ross

Illustrated by
Jennifer Emery

BOYDS MILLS PRESS
HONESDALE, PENNSYLVANIA

GETTING STARTED

The crafts in this book can be made by children of all ages. Some of you will want to read the instructions. Others may prefer to just follow the illustrations.

Before you start, check the materials list to make sure you have everything you need for each craft you plan to make. It's a good idea to have these craft supplies on hand: scissors, crayons, markers, craft glue, cellophane tape, pens, pencils, paint, a hole punch, and a stapler. These items are used so frequently in these projects that we don't include them in the lists of materials.

Use old newspapers, brown paper from grocery bags, or an old sheet or vinyl tablecloth to cover your work area. Protect your clothes with a smock, or wear old clothes you won't mind getting messy. And, speaking of messy, be sure to clean up when you have finished.

While the pictures and instructions are helpful guides, don't forget to use your imagination to add the touches—glitter or beads, crayons or paint—that will make each craft your own. Above all, have fun!

CONTENTS

Getting Started 5
Squirrel Message Can 8
Fall Leaf Coasters 10
Changing-Leaves Tree 12
Apple Zipper Fob 14
Polka-Dot Pen Holder 16
Woolly Bear Caterpillar Race 18
Monarch Butterfly Puppet 20
Columbus Day Ships 22
Keep-Your-Place Bookmark 24
Moody Jack 26
Bat Treat Holder 28
Black Cat Table Decoration 30
Ghosts Pin 32
Flag Magnet 34
Crow Stabile 36
Turkey Favor 38
Canoe Place Card 40
Pilgrim Tissue Box 42
Football Kicker Puppet 44
Good Night, Mr. Bear 46

KEEP IMPORTANT NOTES IN ONE PLACE

SQUIRREL MESSAGE CAN

HERE IS WHAT YOU NEED

- brown chenille stick
- old puzzle piece shaped like this
- 1-inch brown pompom
- 1/4-inch brown pompom
- brown felt scrap
- two tiny wiggle eyes
- brown seed bead
- magnetic strip
- clean soup can with the label removed
- brown construction paper

HERE IS WHAT YOU DO

1 Cut a 1-inch piece of brown chenille stick for the squirrel's tail. Lay the puzzle piece plain side up. Glue the chenille stick so that one end curves up from one of the rounded knobs of the puzzle piece.

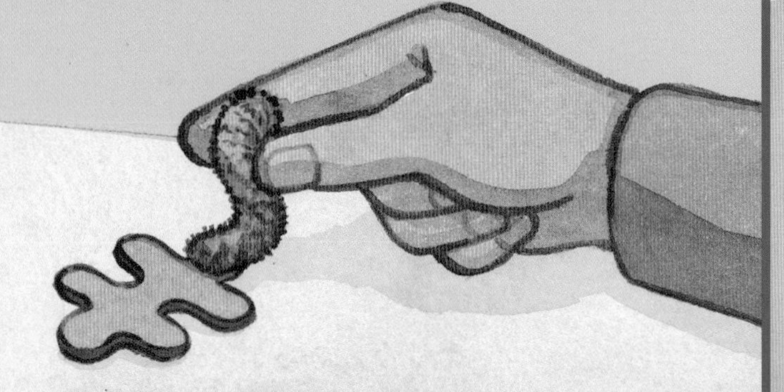

2 Snip fuzz from the side of the 1-inch pompom. Glue the fuzz to cover the puzzle piece for the squirrel's body.

3 Glue the 1/4-inch brown pompom to the end opposite the tail to make the squirrel's head. Cut tiny ears from the brown felt scrap and glue them to the top of the head. Glue the wiggle eyes to the head below the ears. Glue the seed-bead nose below the eyes. Glue a magnetic strip to the bottom of the puzzle piece.

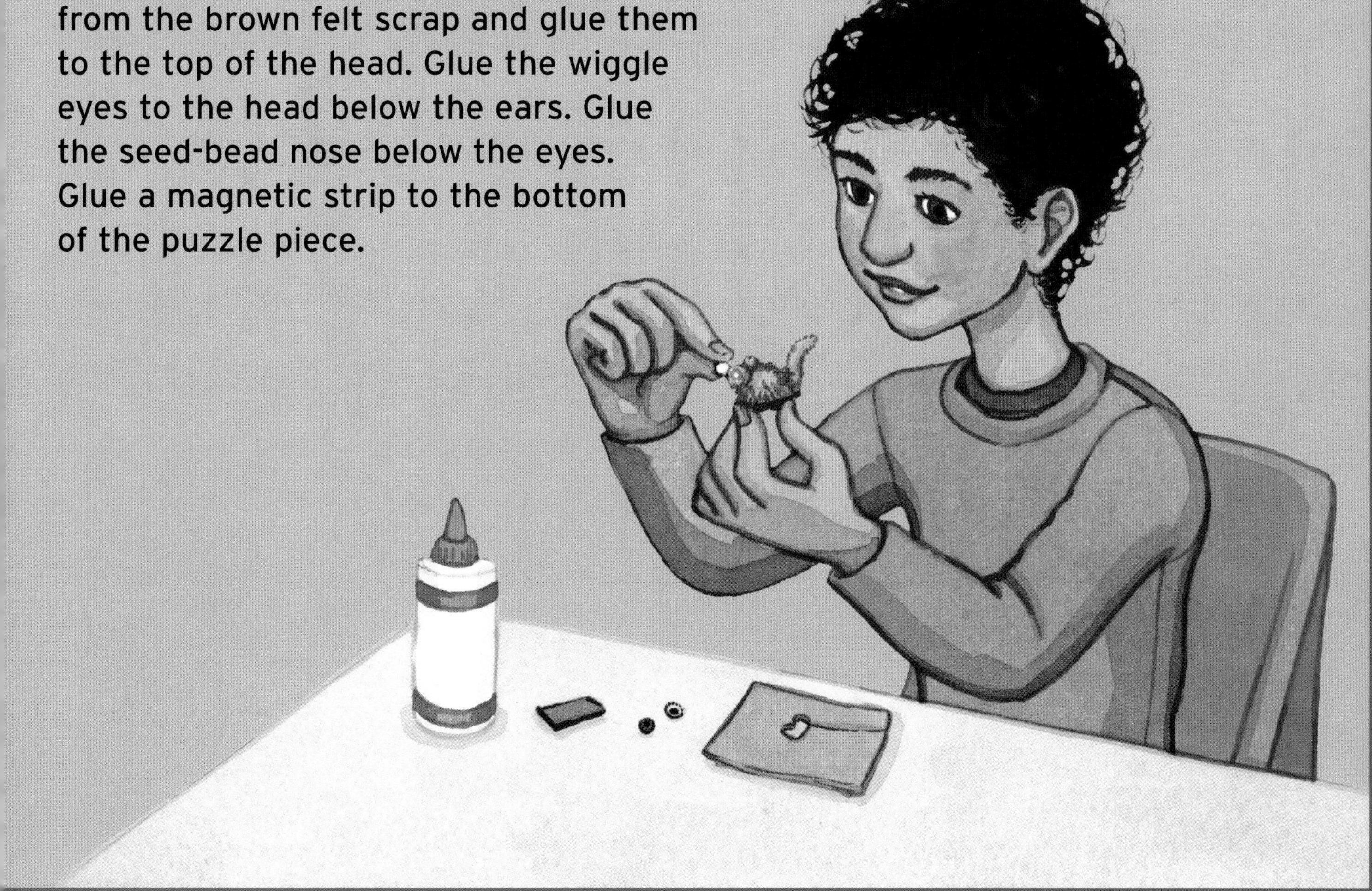

4 Cover the soup can with brown construction paper and secure with tape. Use a marker to draw lines on the paper to make it look like tree bark.

Place a pencil and pieces of scrap paper inside the can. Stick the squirrel on the outside of the can to hold messages.

SET A HARVEST TABLE

FALL LEAF COASTERS

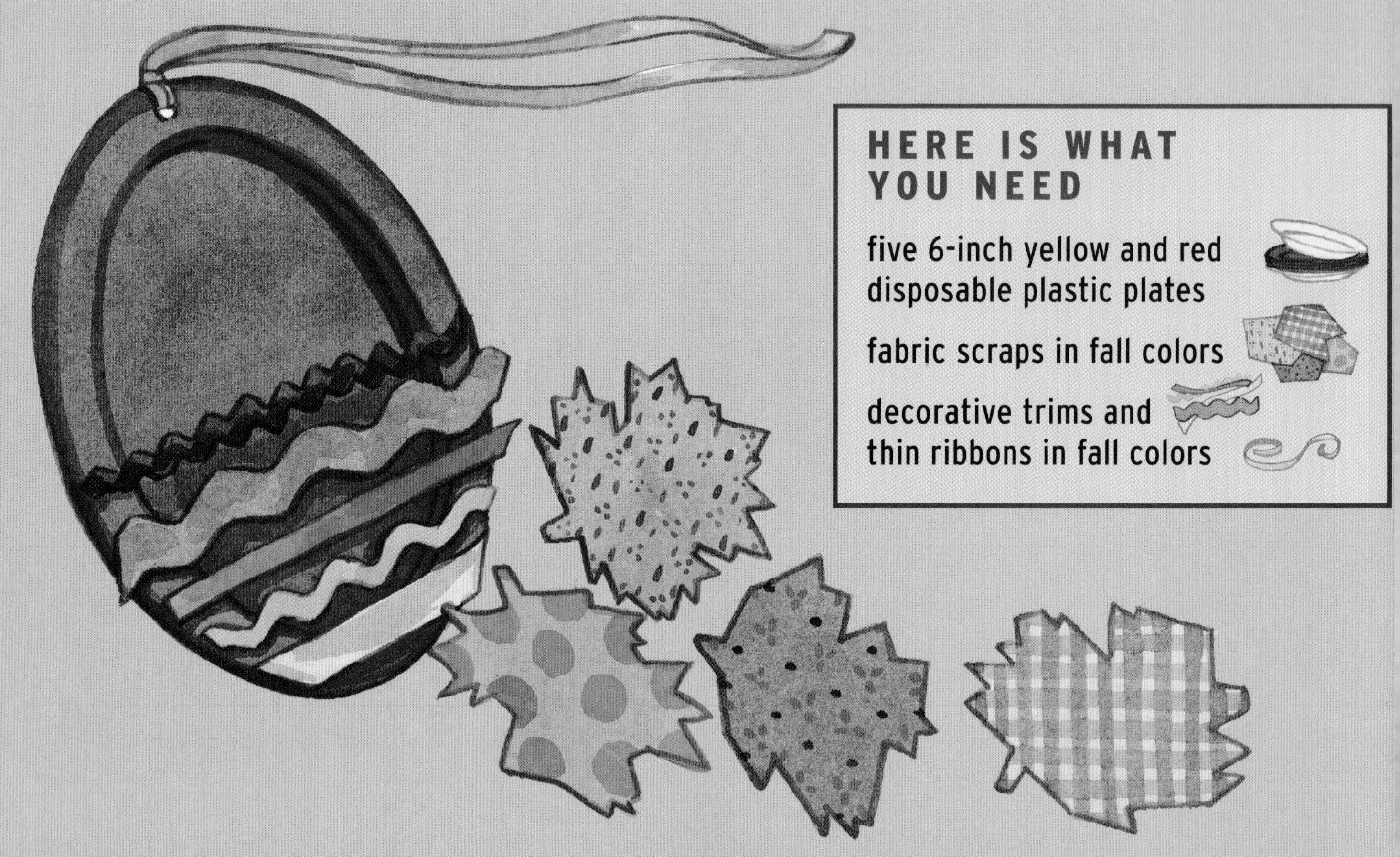

HERE IS WHAT YOU NEED

- five 6-inch yellow and red disposable plastic plates
- fabric scraps in fall colors
- decorative trims and thin ribbons in fall colors

HERE IS WHAT YOU DO

1. Draw a leaf shape on the bottom of four plates. (You might want to use a real leaf for a pattern.) Cut the rim off each plate.

2. Glue a square of fabric to each plate on the side opposite the traced leaf. Let dry. Carefully cut out each leaf coaster.

3 To make a holder for the coasters, glue strips of decorative trims and ribbons, from rim to rim, across the bottom half of the remaining plate. Punch a hole in the top of the plate.

4 Cut a foot-long piece of ribbon. Knot the ends together. Fold the ribbon in half and thread the folded center through the hole in the plate. Thread the knotted end through the fold, and pull tight to create a hanger.

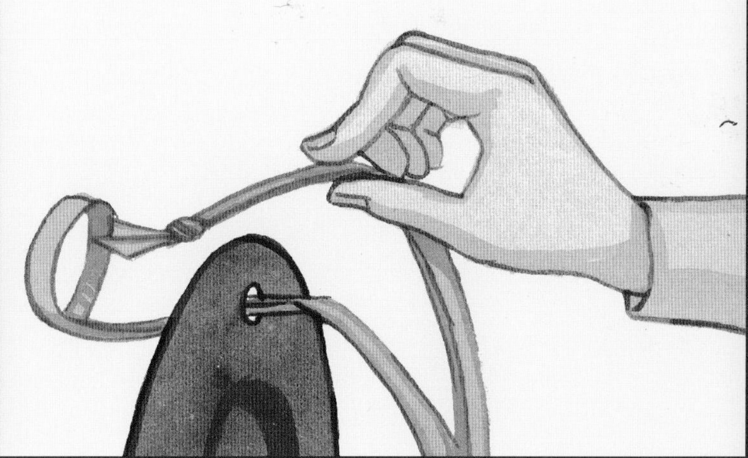

5 Slide the four coasters into the holder and hang the holder on the wall.

These coasters are pretty enough to display all season.

CHANGING-LEAVES TREE

HERE IS WHAT YOU NEED

- old catalogs and magazines with outdoor pictures
- two 9-inch uncoated paper plates
- thin green ribbon
- brown construction paper

HERE IS WHAT YOU DO

1. In the catalogs and magazines, look for pictures of green vegetation and golden, red, and brown vegetation. Tear the pictures out, making two separate piles.

2 Cover the front of one paper plate with a collage of green pictures. Cover the front of the second paper plate with a collage of pictures in fall colors. Punch a hole in the edge of both plates.

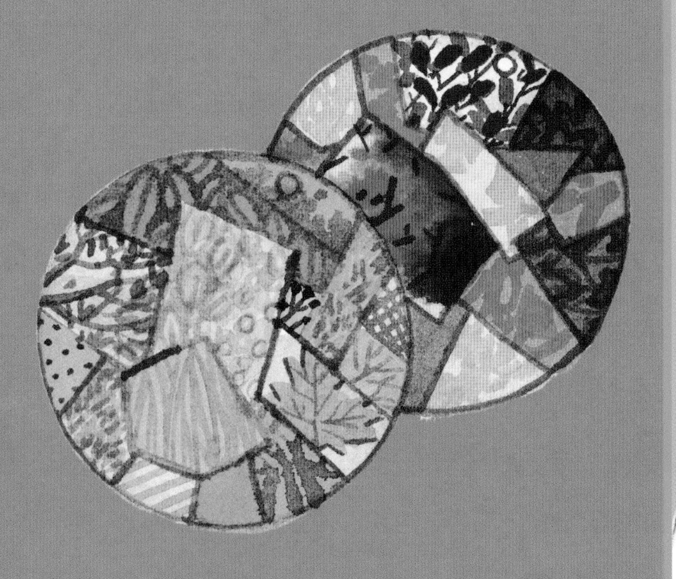

3 Cut a 6-inch piece of the green ribbon. With holes lined up, place the green plate on top of the second plate. Thread the ribbon through the holes and knot the ends together, making sure the ribbon is loose enough so that the green plate will flip behind the second plate easily. Trim off any excess ribbon.

4 Cut a tree trunk from the brown construction paper. Glue the top of the trunk behind the plate with the fall colors.

Hang the tree by the ribbon. To change the tree from summer to autumn, flip the green plate behind the plate with the fall colors. You might want to add a spring and winter plate to your changing tree.

ADD A JINGLE TO A JACKET OR BACKPACK

APPLE ZIPPER FOB

HERE IS WHAT YOU NEED

- 1-inch jingle bell
- large paper clip
- two tiny wiggle eyes
- tiny green pompom
- brown chenille stick
- green felt scrap

HERE IS WHAT YOU DO

1. Slip the jingle bell on one end of the paper clip. Holding the jingle bell by the paper clip, paint the bell red. Let dry.

2 Glue the two wiggle eyes and the pompom to one side for the face. The split in the jingle bell should form the smile.

3 To make a stem, cut a 1-inch piece of brown chenille stick. Slide it through the loop at the top of the jingle bell. Twist the two ends together to secure, and trim off any excess.

4 Cut a tiny leaf from the green felt scrap. Glue the leaf to the top of the jingle bell next to the stem.

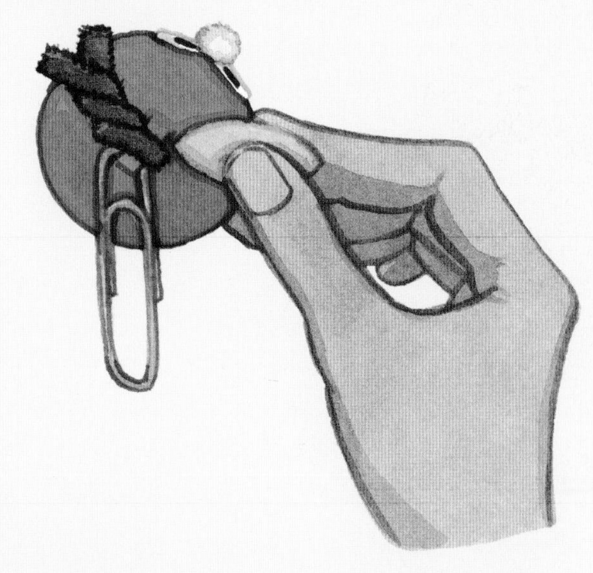

To attach the zipper fob, slip the open end of the paper clip through the hole on a zipper tab.

ORGANIZE YOUR DESK

POLKA-DOT PEN HOLDER

HERE IS WHAT YOU NEED

- 2-inch plastic-foam ball
- 2$1/2$-inch-wide plastic lid
- ballpoint pen
- aluminum foil
- felt scrap
- ribbon, rickrack, or other decorative trim
- colorful thumbtacks

HERE IS WHAT YOU DO

1 **Ask an adult to help you** cut a little less than half off the plastic-foam ball. Put the smaller piece aside for another craft.

2 Glue the flat side of the plastic foam to the inside of the plastic lid. Let dry. Push the ballpoint pen into the ball to create a hole to hold the pen.

3 Cover the ball and the sides of the lid with aluminum foil, folding the edges under and trimming off the excess foil. Use the pen to trace around the lid on the felt scrap. Cut out the circle. Glue it on the bottom of the lid to conceal the foil edges. Glue decorative trim around the holder.

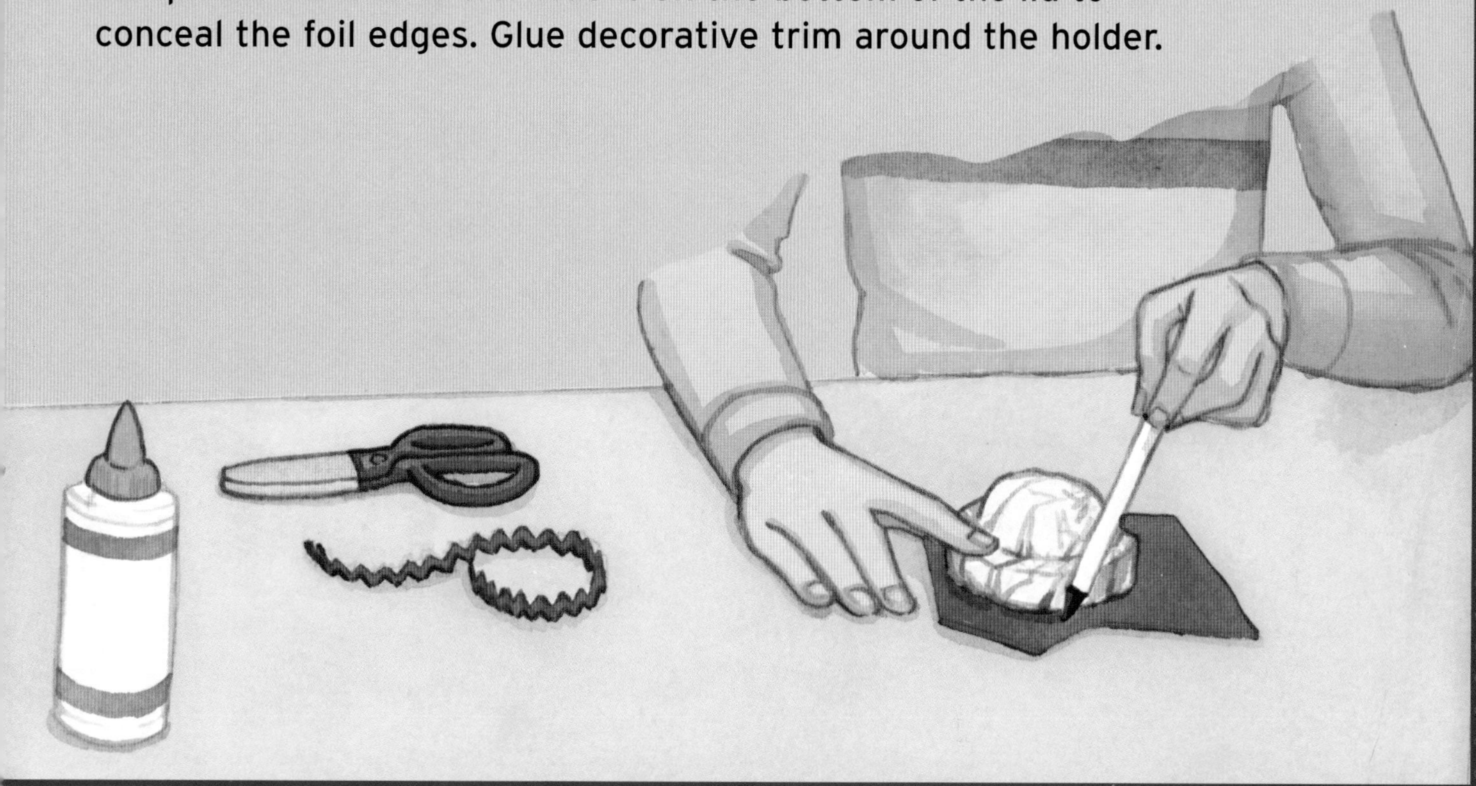

4 Run your finger over the foil to find the hole. Push the pen through the foil into the hole. Decorate the holder with thumbtacks.

Now you are ready to do your schoolwork!

CHALLENGE YOUR FRIENDS

WOOLLY BEAR CATERPILLAR RACE

HERE IS WHAT YOU NEED

- cardboard paper towel tube
- pennies
- masking tape
- drinking straws

HERE IS WHAT YOU DO

1. Cut a 1-inch-wide ring from the cardboard tube. If the ring starts to come apart at any point, secure it with glue.

2. Cut across the ring to open it. Round off the corners on both sides of the cut.

3 Pull the tube open slightly and bend out a 1-inch piece at each end for the head and the tail of the caterpillar. Color the tube to look like an orange-and-black-striped caterpillar.

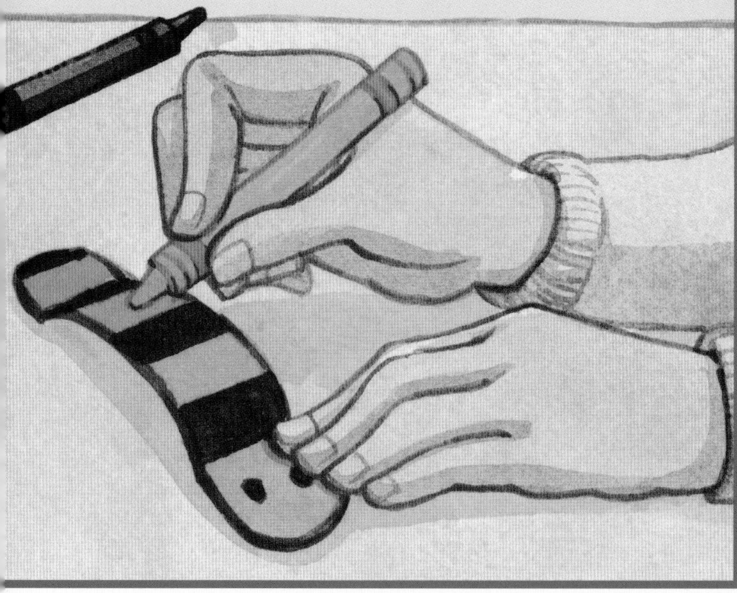

4 Use cellophane tape to attach a penny to the bottom of the head and tail of the caterpillar to add stability to the figure.

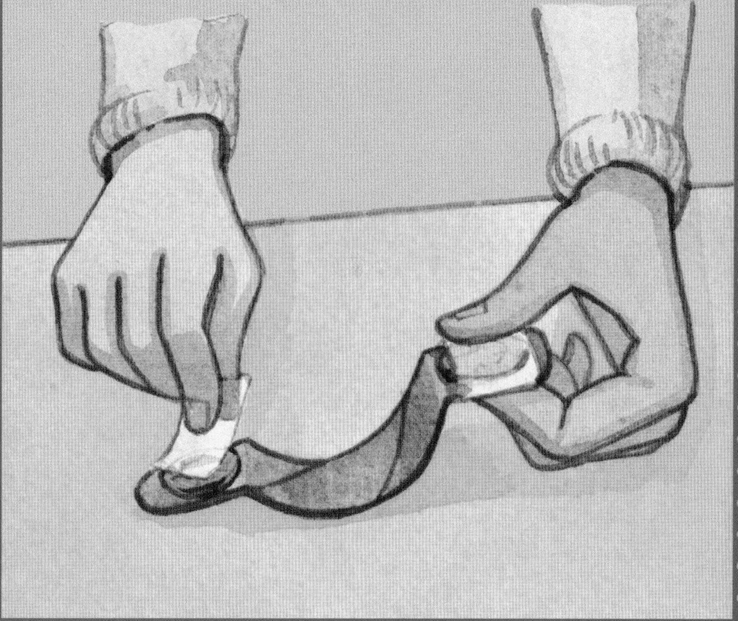

To race the caterpillars, find a smooth surface such as a table. Use masking tape to mark start and finish lines for the race. Take one caterpillar for yourself and assign one to each player. To race, each player must use a drinking straw to blow on his or her caterpillar from behind. The first player to blow the caterpillar across the finish line is the winner.

FINGER FLUTTERER

MONARCH BUTTERFLY PUPPET

To use the puppet, slip the neck of the balloon over your finger. Wiggle it to make the butterfly "fly" south for the winter.

HERE IS WHAT YOU NEED

- 6-inch-round orange balloon
- black chenille stick
- black permanent marker
- brown construction paper
- cotton ball

HERE IS WHAT YOU DO

1. Flatten the balloon and fold it in half. Cut half a heart shape on the fold. Open the balloon back up and spread the two heart shapes apart to form the wings of the butterfly.

2 Cut a 5-inch piece of black chenille stick. Fold the piece in half and place the base of the wings between the two halves. Twist the halves of the chenille stick together to secure, and tip the ends up to look like the antennae. Use the permanent marker to draw black lines on the tops of the wings.

3 Cut a 5-inch pod shape from the brown construction paper. Cut a slit lengthwise across the pod.

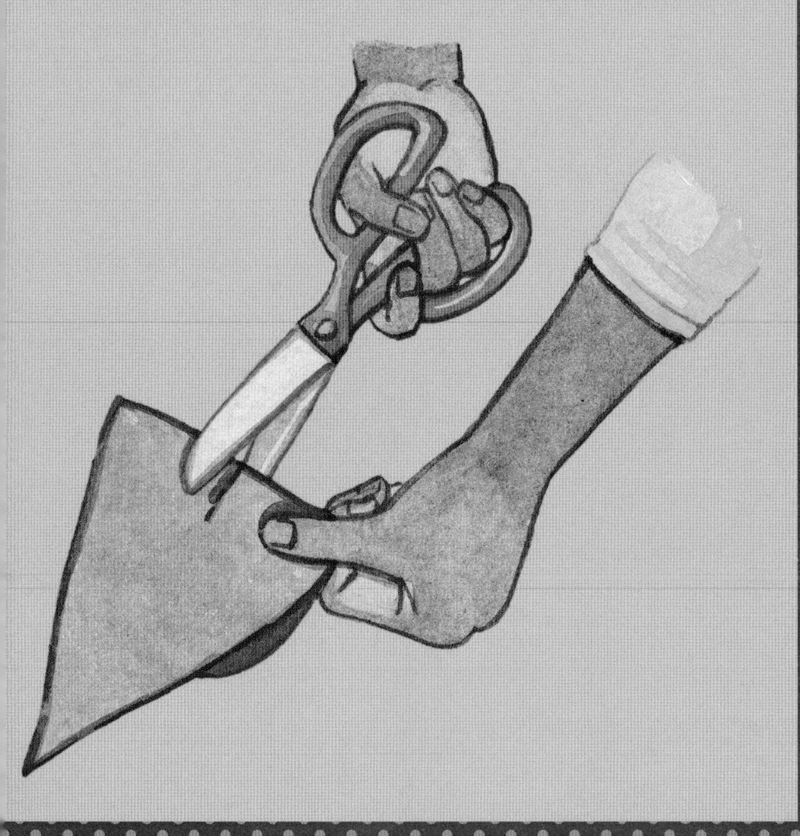

4 Slip the neck of the balloon through the slit in the pod. Glue a small amount of the cotton ball along the slit on top of the pod to look like milkweed seed.

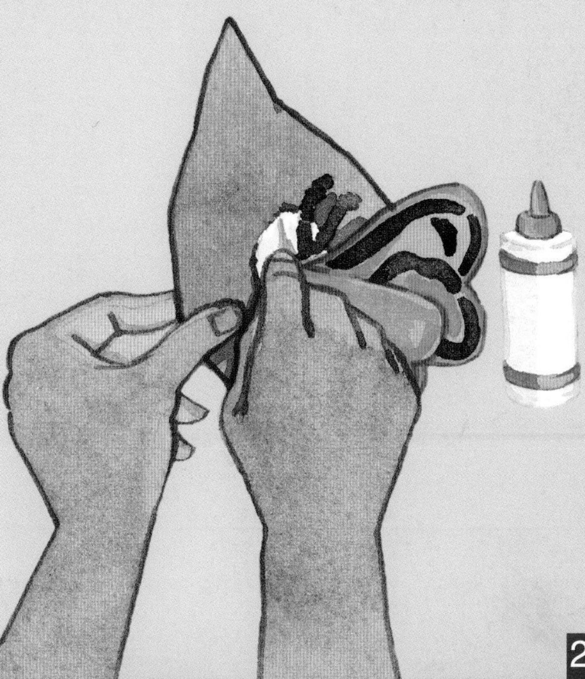

SAIL AWAY

COLUMBUS DAY SHIPS

Set the three ships on the blue "ocean" and they will bob around at the slightest breeze.

HERE IS WHAT YOU NEED

permanent marker

small end of three plastic eggs

old fun dough

chenille stick

white paper towel

red paper scrap

9-inch white paper plate

9-inch blue plastic disposable plate

HERE IS WHAT YOU DO

1. Use the permanent marker to write the name of a ship—*Niña, Pinta,* and *Santa Maria*—on the side of each egg half.

2. Roll three marble-size balls of fun dough. Glue a ball of dough in the bottom of each egg half.

3 Cut three 3-inch pieces of chenille stick for the three ship masts. Cut three 2-inch squares from the white paper towel for the three sails. Cut two slits across each sail. Slide a chenille-stick mast through each sail. Cut three tiny triangle flags from the red paper scrap. Glue a flag to the top of each mast. Dip the bottom of each mast in glue and press one into the dough in each ship.

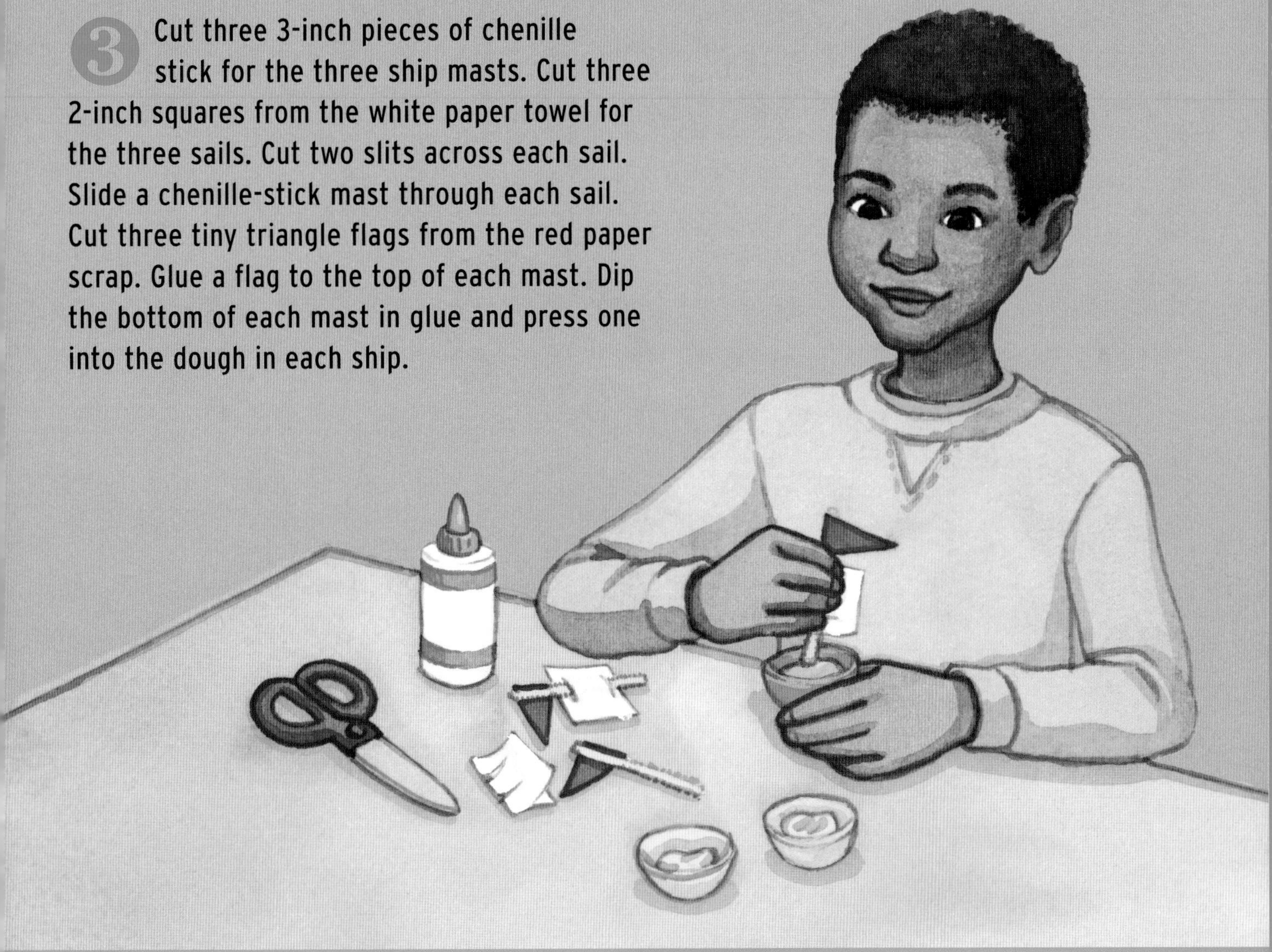

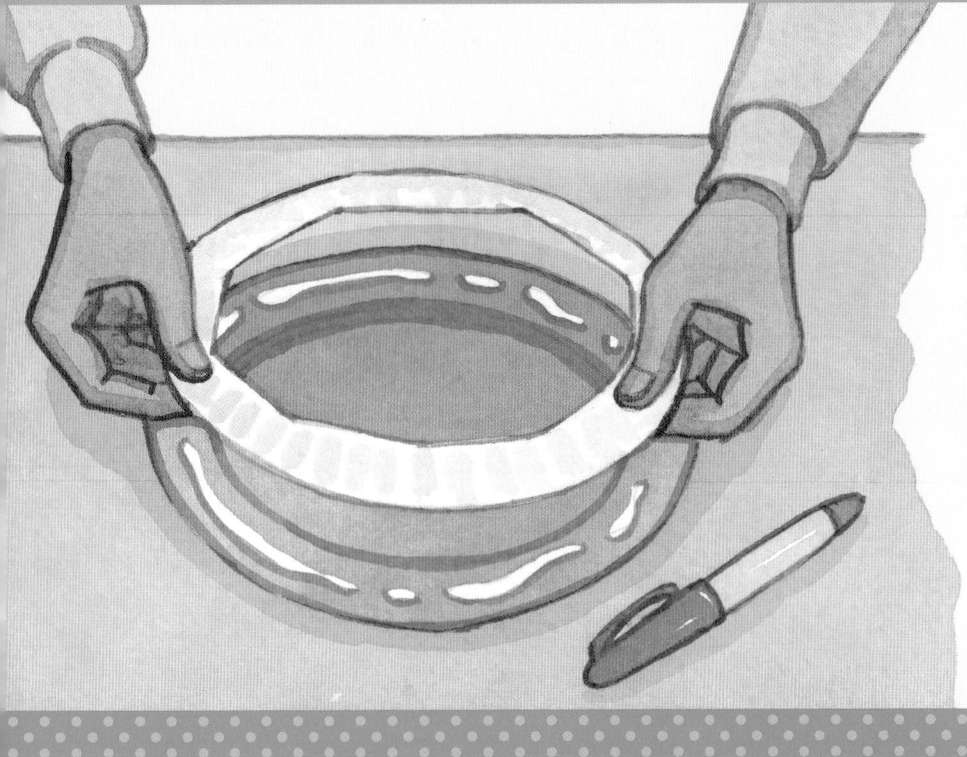

4 Cut the center out of the white plate. Turn the rim over and glue it to the rim of the blue plate. If you wish, write something around the plate rim such as "Happy Columbus Day" or the rhyme "In 1492, Columbus sailed the ocean blue."

FIND WHERE YOU LEFT OFF

KEEP-YOUR-PLACE BOOKMARK

HERE IS WHAT YOU NEED

- poster board
- gift wrap or scrapbook paper
- decorative trim to match the paper

HERE IS WHAT YOU DO

1. Cut a strip of the poster board 10 inches long and $1\frac{1}{2}$ inches wide. Cut a second strip 6 inches long and $1\frac{1}{2}$ inches wide.

2. Glue the gift wrap on both sides of each strip. Make sure the paper is larger than the cardboard strips. Let dry.

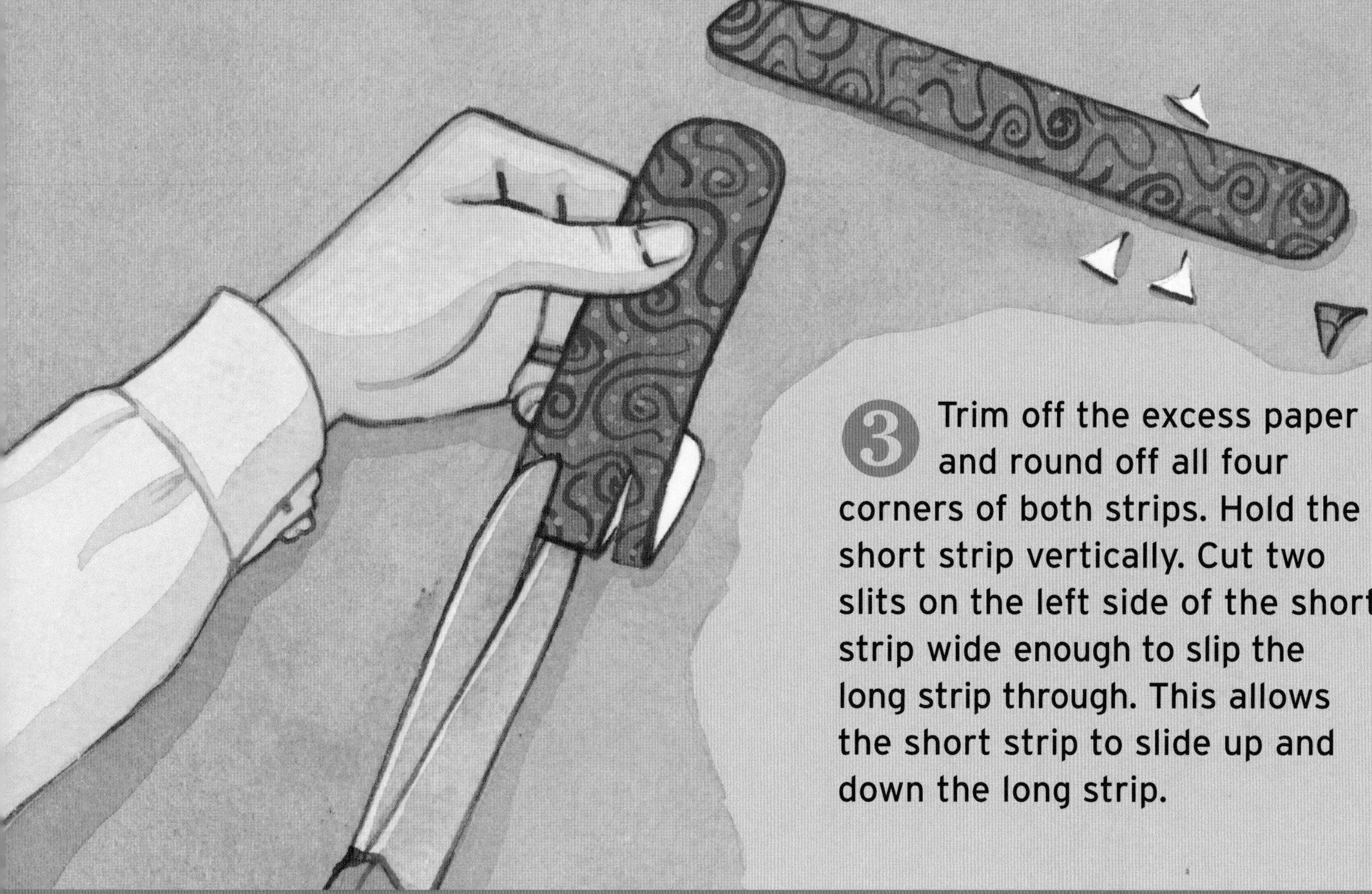

3 Trim off the excess paper and round off all four corners of both strips. Hold the short strip vertically. Cut two slits on the left side of the short strip wide enough to slip the long strip through. This allows the short strip to slide up and down the long strip.

4 Glue a strip of the decorative trim across the short strip. Insert the long strip into the short one.

The sliding strip on the bookmark allows you to mark the place on the page where you left off. The long strip marks the page.

CHANGE FACES IN THE BLINK OF AN EYE

MOODY JACK

HERE IS WHAT YOU NEED

- 3-inch plastic-foam ball
- small plastic lid
- small, flat, square gift box
- green, brown, and black chenille sticks
- green felt scrap
- black craft foam
- ballpoint pen

Store the extra pieces for this changeable jack-o'-lantern inside the box.

HERE IS WHAT YOU DO

1. Paint the plastic-foam ball orange. Let dry.

2. Glue the plastic lid, top side down, to the center of the box lid to create a stand for the pumpkin. Paint the box and lid green. Let dry.

3. Cut an inch-long piece of green chenille stick. Press it into the top of the pumpkin to make a stem. Cut a 3-inch piece of brown chenille stick. Wrap it around your finger to create a twisted vine. Press one end of the vine into the top of the pumpkin, next to the stem. Cut a leaf from the green felt. Snip a tiny hole in one end of the leaf and slide it over the vine.

4. Cut four 1-inch pieces of black chenille stick. Fold each piece in half. Press the ends into the pumpkin where you wish to add eyes, nose, and a mouth, leaving the folded part sticking out.

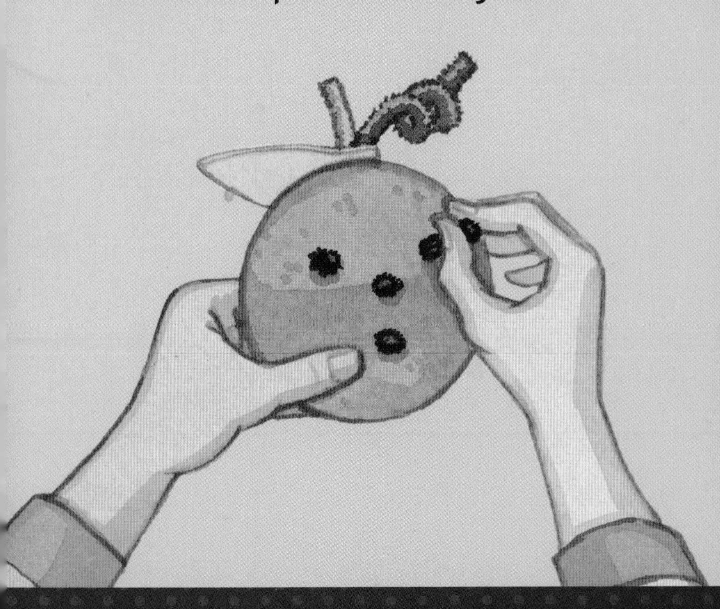

5. Cut a variety of facial features for the pumpkin from the black craft foam. Use a ballpoint pen to poke a tiny hole through the center of each feature. Attach the features to the pumpkin by slipping the hole in each foam piece over a folded chenille stick.

BAT TREAT HOLDER

HERE IS WHAT YOU NEED

- bathroom tissue tube
- paper clips
- two wiggle eyes
- white and black craft foam or construction paper
- metal fastener
- orange ribbon

Fill the bat with candy or small toys to use as a party favor.

HERE IS WHAT YOU DO

1 Pinch one end of the bathroom tissue tube closed. Cut a triangle shape from the end to create pointed ears for the bat. Glue the flattened end closed. Secure with paper clips until the glue dries. Paint the tube black and let dry.

2 Glue two wiggle eyes to the tube. Cut two small triangle-shaped teeth from the white craft foam and glue them below the eyes.

3 Cut two wings from the black craft foam. Attach them to the back of the bat using the metal fastener.

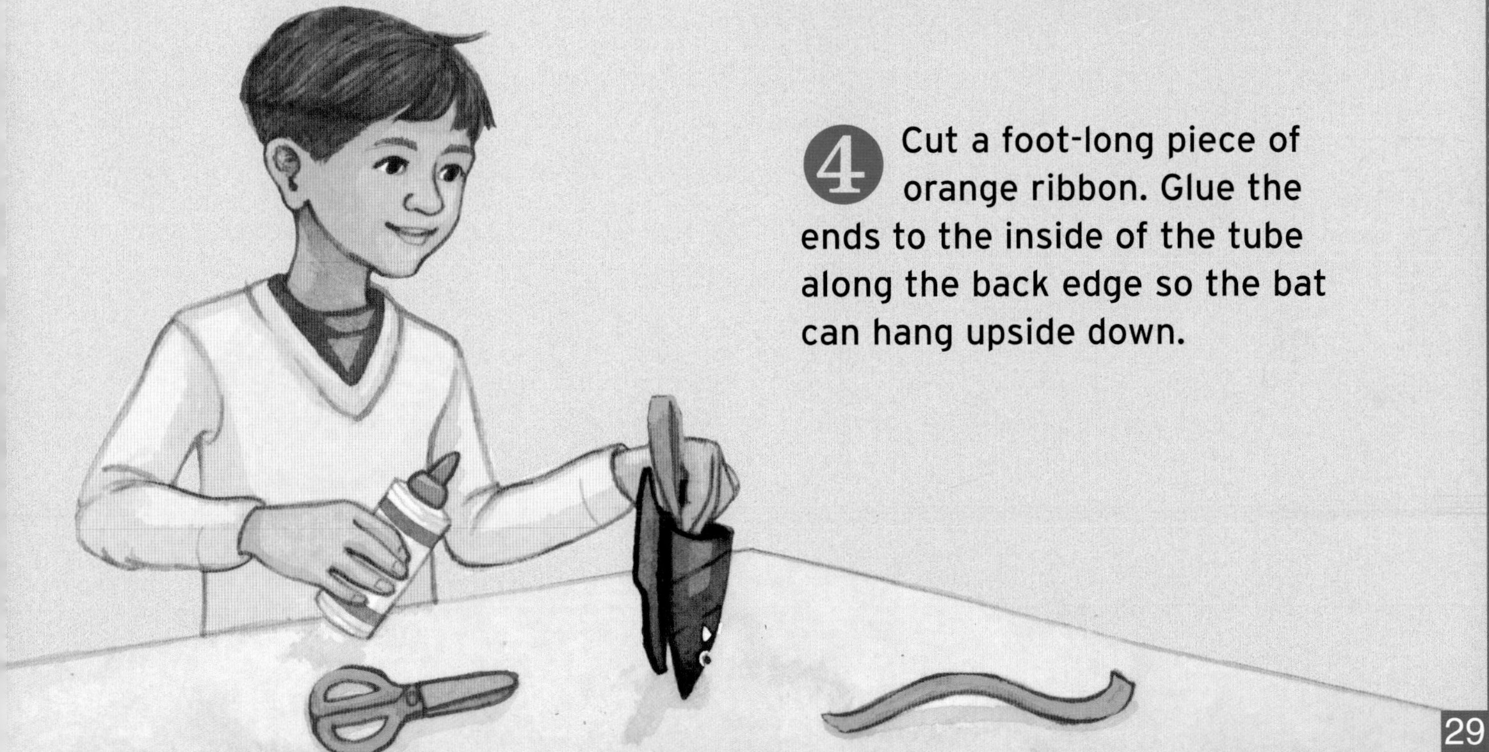

4 Cut a foot-long piece of orange ribbon. Glue the ends to the inside of the tube along the back edge so the bat can hang upside down.

A PURR-FECT HALLOWEEN

BLACK CAT TABLE DECORATION

HERE IS WHAT YOU NEED

- paper towel tube
- two $1\frac{1}{2}$-inch and three 1-inch black pompoms
- black chenille stick
- thin orange ribbon
- white string
- tiny pink pompom
- two wiggle eyes
- black felt scrap

HERE IS WHAT YOU DO

1 Cut off two 1-inch-wide rings from the paper towel tube. Cut each ring open to make a strip. Glue one strip on top of the other, pulling the ends out to make a frame for the arched body of the cat. Paint the frame black and let dry.

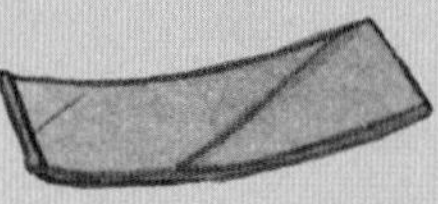

2. Glue the two large pompoms under the arched body frame.

3. Cut a 3-inch piece of black chenille stick for the tail. Poke a hole in one end of the frame. Glue the end of the chenille-stick piece in the hole. Tie an orange bow around the tail.

4. Glue two of the smaller black pompoms side by side to the other end of the body. Glue the third one in the center above the other two to form the head.

5. Cut three 3-inch pieces of white string. Knot them together at the center to make whiskers. Glue the whiskers to the head. Add the pink pompom over the knot for a nose. Glue the two wiggle eyes above the nose. Cut two triangle-shaped ears from the black felt. Glue the ears above the eyes. Make a bow from the orange ribbon and glue it below the head.

Add this cat to a centerpiece, or display it on a shelf.

FLOATS ON A COAT

GHOSTS PIN

HERE IS WHAT YOU NEED

two white twist ties

white plastic grocery bag

black permanent marker

jewelry pin-back

You can make this pin with only one ghost or several glued together.

HERE IS WHAT YOU DO

1. Bend each white twist tie into a U-shape. Rub glue along the entire inside of one of the folded twist ties.

2. Place your finger inside the grocery bag at a place that is entirely white and has no writing. Glue the twist tie to the bag over your finger so that the bag puffs out and forms a ghost shape.

3 Glue the second twist tie to the bag in the same way. When the glue has dried, completely cut around the ghosts to remove them from the bag.

4 Use the black permanent marker to create a face for each ghost. Glue the two ghosts together side by side.

5 Glue the jewelry pin-back to the back of the ghosts where they are joined together.

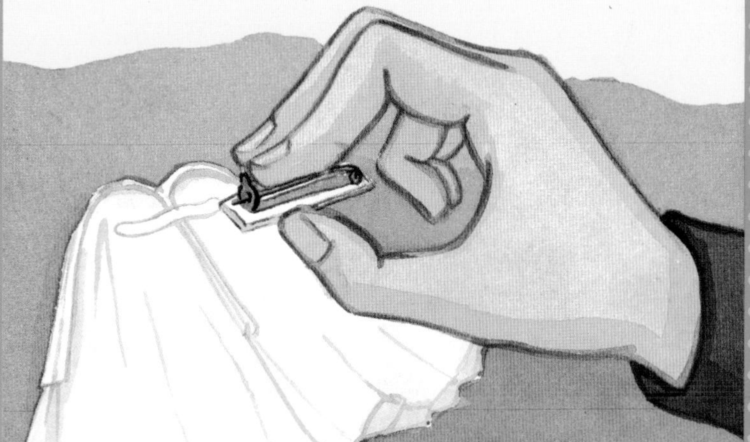

FLY THE RED, WHITE, AND BLUE FOR VETERANS DAY

FLAG MAGNET

HERE IS WHAT YOU NEED

corrugated cardboard

blue construction paper

gold glitter

magnetic strip

HERE IS WHAT YOU DO

1. Cut a rectangle from the corrugated cardboard that has seven bumps for the seven red stripes. Paint the cardboard white and let dry. Color or paint each of the bumps red, leaving the space in between the bumps white. Let dry.

2 Cut a rectangle from the blue construction paper that will cover four of the stripes on the upper left-hand corner of the flag. Glue the blue rectangle in place.

3 Cut a paper rectangle the size of your flag and glue it to the back.

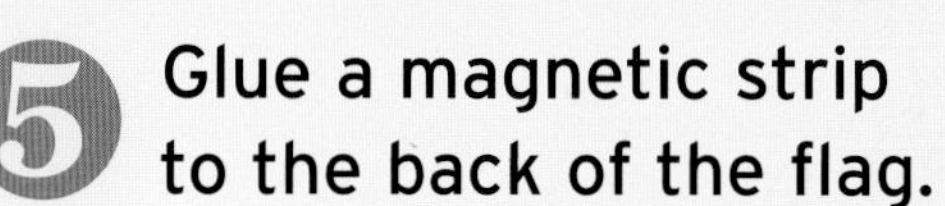

4 Spread glue to cover the blue paper and sprinkle with the gold glitter to make the stars.

5 Glue a magnetic strip to the back of the flag.

Change the magnetic strip to a jewelry pin-back and wear the flag on your jacket.

CAWS IN THE CORN

CROW STABILE

HERE IS WHAT YOU NEED

colorful 8-ounce paper or plastic cup

ribbon, rickrack, or other decorative trim

2-inch plastic-foam ball

five 12-inch yellow chenille sticks

pony beads (15 black, about 30 yellow)

ten tiny wiggle eyes

black construction paper

HERE IS WHAT YOU DO

1. Cut the cup down to about half the original height. Glue decorative trim around the outer rim. Glue the plastic-foam ball inside the cup.

2 To make each of the five crows, bend one end of a yellow chenille stick about 1 inch. Slide three black pony beads on the stick for the body, leaving the end of the chenille stick for the beak. Glue two tiny wiggle eyes to the bead closest to the beak. Cut wings and a tail from the black construction paper and glue them in place.

3 Stick the end of each chenille stick into the ball so it looks as if the crows are flying above the cup.

4 Cover the top of the ball with glue. Place yellow pony beads in the glue to look like corn.

Wiggle the base of the stabile and watch the crows fly.

HOLD THANKSGIVING GOODIES

TURKEY FAVOR

Guests will love to find this turkey next to their plates at the table.

HERE IS WHAT YOU NEED

- ten colorful 12-inch chenille sticks
- orange felt scrap
- two tiny wiggle eyes
- red rickrack
- plastic sandwich bag
- small piece of chenille stick

HERE IS WHAT YOU DO

1. Twist the ends of the ten chenille sticks together at one end until they are twisted together for about 2 inches. Bend the twisted portion in half to form the head of the turkey. Twist the chenille sticks together again once about 4 inches from the end opposite the head. Bend the ends up and fan them out to form the tail.

2 Hold the head and the base of the tail and gently press them toward each other to spread out the center of the sticks to form the body. Arrange the sticks of the body and the tail so that they are evenly spaced.

3 Cut a triangle beak for the turkey from the orange felt. Glue the beak to the end of the head. Glue the two wiggle eyes to the head above the beak.

4 Cut a 1-inch piece of red rickrack for the wattle. Glue the end of the rickrack across the top of the beak. Let the other end hang down the side.

5 Fill the plastic sandwich bag with candies. Wrap the small piece of chenille stick around the opening. Tuck the bag of goodies inside the body of the turkey.

MARK EVERYONE'S SEAT AT THE TABLE

CANOE PLACE CARD

Put a place card above each plate when you set the table.

HERE IS WHAT YOU NEED

- flexible-fabric adhesive bandage
- blue construction paper
- cotton swab
- rickrack or other decorative trim

HERE IS WHAT YOU DO

1 Fold the adhesive bandage in half lengthwise. Stick the sides on each end together to create a canoe. Draw decorations on both sides of the canoe. You might want to decorate any additional canoes before you fold them, once you know what the folded canoe will look like.

2 Cut a 2-by-$3\frac{1}{2}$-inch rectangle of blue construction paper.

3 To make the paddle, cut a 1-inch piece from one end of a cotton swab and paint it brown. Let dry.

4 Glue the canoe along the top left-hand corner of the place card. Glue a strip of rickrack across the bottom of the card. Glue the handle of the paddle to the canoe. Glue the other end to the card. Use markers to write the name of a guest on the place card.

STOP THE SNIFFLES

PILGRIM TISSUE BOX

HERE IS WHAT YOU NEED

square-shaped box of tissues

black, skin-toned, and white construction paper

thin blue ribbon

yarn bits

Display the tissue box on the edge of a shelf with the apron hanging down. When a tissue apron is pulled out, another will replace it.

HERE IS WHAT YOU DO

1. Turn the tissue box on one side so that the tissue hangs down to form the apron for the Pilgrim. Cut a flared skirt from the black construction paper and glue it to the box under the apron. Cut two rectangle sleeves from the black paper. Glue the sleeves to the box above the apron so that they stick out on each side.

2 Cut two hands and a head from the skin-toned paper. Cut cuffs and a collar from the white paper. Glue a cuff over the end of each sleeve. Glue a hand sticking out from behind each cuff. Glue the collar to the center of the Pilgrim above the apron. Glue the head to the top of the collar.

3 Cut three thin rectangles from the white paper. Glue them to the sides and top of the head to form the hat. Make a small bow from the blue ribbon. Glue the bow at the neck of the Pilgrim.

4 Glue yarn bits around the inside of the hat. Use markers to add facial features. Pull a tissue over the dress to form the apron.

SCORE A FIELD GOAL

FOOTBALL KICKER PUPPET

HERE IS WHAT YOU NEED

- poster board
- old stretchy glove
- felt scraps
- two wiggle eyes
- cardboard egg carton
- three craft sticks
- 1-inch brown pompom

HERE IS WHAT YOU DO

1. Draw a simple 5-inch figure on the poster board. Cut out the figure. If you are right-handed, cut about an inch off the figure's left leg. If you are left-handed, cut an inch off the figure's right leg. Cut two fingers from the glove. Slip a finger over each leg and glue it to the front of each leg. Be sure not to glue the glove fingers closed.

2 Turn the figure over. Trace around the figure on felt to make a football shirt, pants, and helmet. Glue them on the front of the figure. Add details to the uniform, such as stripes and a number, from felt. Use markers to draw a mouth and nose. Glue on the two wiggle eyes to complete the face.

3 Cut two cups from the cardboard egg carton. Paint them if you wish. Turn the cups upside down and cut a slit in the top of each. Dip the end of a craft stick in glue and slide it down into the slit in the cup. Do the same with the second stick and cup. Glue the third stick across the two sticks to make the goalposts.

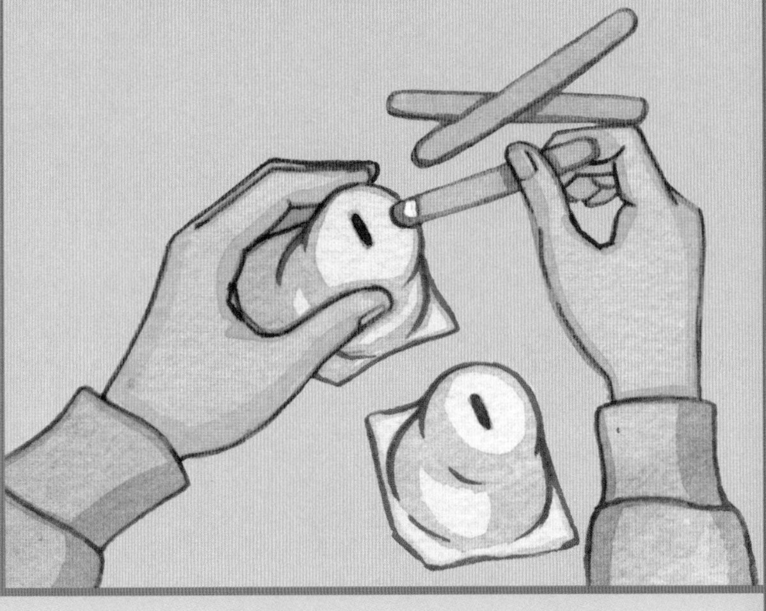

4 Trim the brown pompom into a football shape by snipping fuzz off the sides. (Do not cut through the center, or it will come apart.)

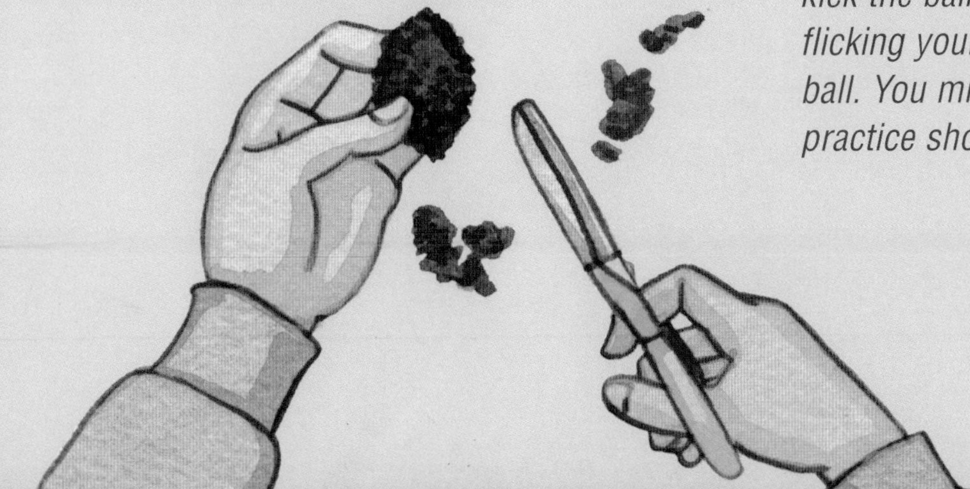

To use the puppet, place your pointer finger in the glove finger with the cut leg and your middle finger in the other leg. Hold your other hand flat and set the football on it. Make the puppet kick the ball through the goalposts by flicking your pointer finger against the ball. You might need to take some practice shots before you score.

TUCK HIM INTO HIS COZY DEN

GOODNIGHT, MR. BEAR

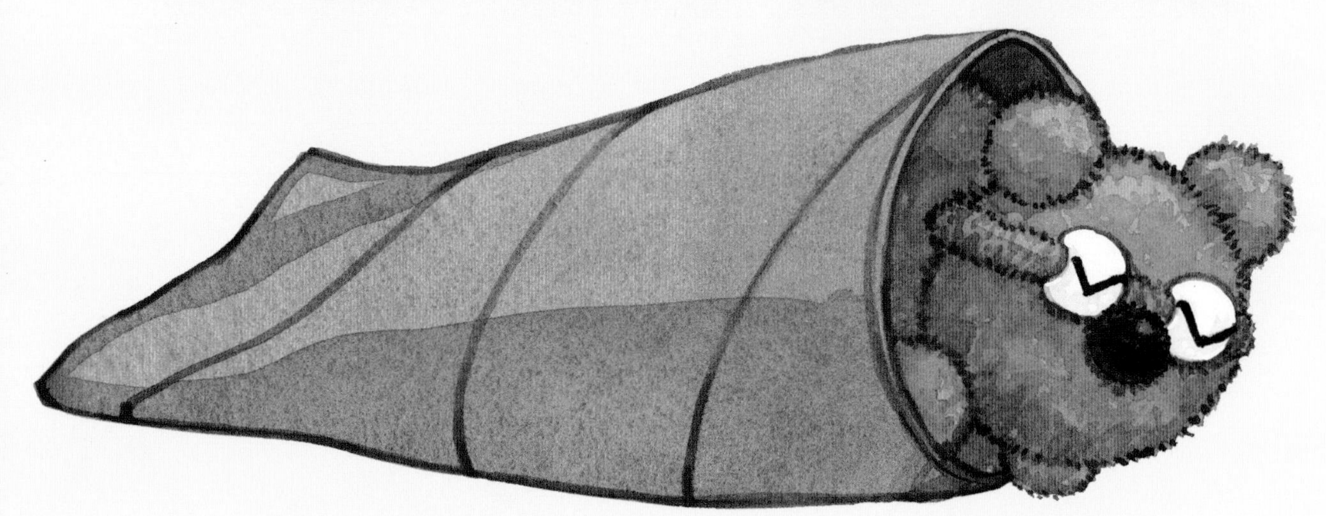

Roll the bear's eyes shut and slip him into the cave for a nap. Wake up the bear by rolling his eyes to the open side.

HERE IS WHAT YOU NEED

- two white pony beads
- brown chenille stick
- black permanent marker 
- 1-inch brown pompom
- tiny black pompom
- six 1/4-inch brown pompoms
- 2-inch brown pompom
- bathroom tissue tube 
- paper clips 

HERE IS WHAT YOU DO

1 String the two pony beads onto a 3-inch piece of brown chenille stick. Use the black permanent marker to draw an open eye on one side of each bead and a closed eye on the opposite side.

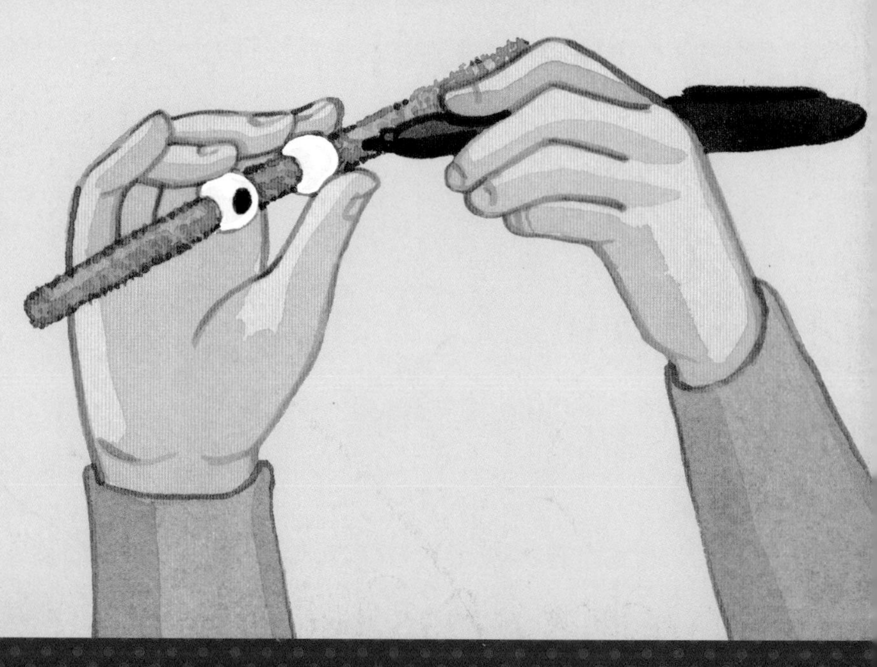

2 Wrap the chenille stick lightly around the middle of the 1-inch brown pompom. The beads should be close together. Twist the ends of the chenille stick together to secure, and trim off any excess. Spread the two bead eyes apart just enough to glue the black pompom below the chenille stick and between the eyes. Glue two 1/4-inch brown pompoms to the top of the head for ears.

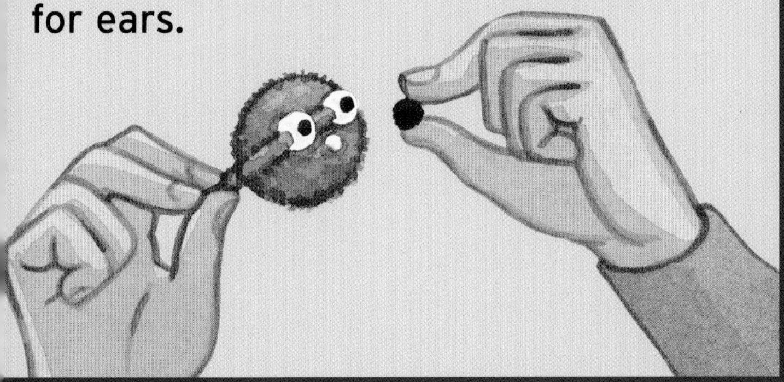

3 Glue the head to the 2-inch brown pompom, which will be the body. Glue the last four 1/4-inch pompoms to the bottom of the body for the legs.

4 To make a cave for the bear, cut a 3 1/2-inch piece from the bathroom tissue tube. Flatten one end of the tube and secure with glue. Use paper clips to hold the sides together until the glue dries.

For Julianna and Ashlyn
—K. R.

Boyds Mills Press, Inc.
A Highlights Company
815 Church Street
Honesdale, Pennsylvania 18431
Printed in China

Library of Congress Cataloging-in-Publication Data

Ross, Kathy (Katharine Reynolds).
Step-by-step crafts for fall / by Kathy Ross ; illustrated by Jennifer Emery.—1st ed.
p. cm.
ISBN-13: 978-1-59078-357-3 (pbk. : alk. paper)
ISBN-13: 978-1-59078-448-8 (hardcover : alk. paper)
1. Handicraft—Juvenile literature. I. Emery, Jennifer. II. Title.

TT160.R714237 2006
745.5—dc22

2006010003

First edition, 2006
The text of this book is set in 14-point Interstate Regular.
The illustrations are done in watercolor.
Visit our Web site at www.boydsmillspress.com

10 9 8 7 6 5 4 3 2 1 hc
10 9 8 7 6 5 4 3 2 1 pb